Where Is Jesus?

Luke 2:41–52 for children

Jonathan Schkade

Illustrated by Linda Pierce

CONCORDIA PUBLISHING HOUSE · SAINT LOUIS

You've all heard of Jesus,
God's own precious Son,
Born unto me, Mary,
To save everyone.

I raised Him in Nazareth.
He learned and He knew
About God and His Word
And all that was true.

But when He was twelve years,
I took Jesus down
With our friends and with Joseph
To Jerusalem town.

That week in the city,
Our bread had no leaven
While we sang and prayed to
The great King of heaven.

But then it was over,
So our hometown group
Came once more together
To Nazareth to troop.

There were so many friends
And family in dozens.
We figured our Jesus
Was off with His cousins.

As fast as my feet could,
With Joseph I hurried
Once more to the city
While horribly worried.

During three awful days,
We searched without finding
In homes, stalls, and alleys.
Our failure was blinding.

At the end of that time,
Quite unsure what to do,
We went to the temple,
Where my joy sprang anew.

Right there with the teachers
Of God's Word so wise,
My Jesus was sitting
Before my own eyes.

He wasn't just listening,
But answering too,
Amazing the teachers
By how much He knew.

I spoke without thinking,
"Son, why were You here
While Your father and I
Sought You both far and near?"

"Why were you out looking?"
He asked me and my spouse.
"Did you not know I'd be
Inside My Father's house?"

Though we were confused by
The answers we'd heard,
Our Jesus came with us,
Obeying our word.

Then Jesus grew daily
In wisdom and might
While inside I treasured
Each sound and each sight.

I wish I had known then
What's now very clear:
Jesus lives for His Father,
Serving Him without fear.

Dear Parent,

In that nightmare moment when a mother realizes that her child is missing, her thoughts might be divided between disbelief ("but he *has* to be here!"), to irritation ("where has he gotten off to?"), to fear ("has something awful happened?"). It's easy to read this Bible story from our own emotional perspective and overlook its significant aspects.

First, this story includes the first words Jesus speaks in the Bible: "Why were you looking for Me? Did you not know that I must be in My Father's house?" (Luke 2:49). This account, the only glimpse of Jesus' childhood we have, draws our attention to His knowledge of the Scriptures and to His obedience to His parents. Second, this account tells us that Jesus, even as a child, always knew and was obedient to His mission. He came to do His Father's will. His response to Mary also shows us that the people who were closest to Him, here and throughout His earthly ministry, didn't quite comprehend who He really was.

The third lesson we can take from this Bible story is that it points to the Passion Narrative—Jesus is gone for three days, but His destination is His Father's house. Like all of Scripture, the story of Jesus in the temple teaches us who He is and what He does for us.

As you read this Arch Book with your child, point out Jesus' knowledge of the Scriptures and His obedience to God's will. We can compare His time of learning to our own.

The editor